Who Invented the Periodic Table?

Nigel Saunders

W
FRANKLIN WATTS
LONDON · SYDNEY

First published in 2010 by Franklin Watts

Copyright © 2010 Arcturus Publishing Limited

Franklin Watts
338 Euston Road
London NW1 3BH

Franklin Watts Australia
Level 17/207 Kent Street, Sydney, NSW 2000

Produced by Arcturus Publishing Limited,
26/27 Bickels Yard, 151–153 Bermondsey Street, London SE1 3HA

The right of Nigel Saunders to be identified as the author of this work has been asserted by him in accordance with the Copyright, Designs and Patents Act 1988.

Planned and produced by Discovery Books Ltd., 2 College Street, Ludlow, Shropshire, SY8 1AN www.discoverybooks.net
Managing editor: Laura Durman
Editor: Penny Worms
Designer: Ian Winton
Illustrator: Stefan Chabluk

Picture Credits
Corbis: cover (Steve Allen/Brand X), 13 (Stefano Bianchetti), 16 (Bettmann), 35 (Bettmann), 36, 38 top (Hulton-Deutsch Collection), 40 (Peter Ginter/Science Faction).
Getty Images: 21 (SSPL).
IBM Corporation: 30.
iStockphoto: 14, 23 bottom (Mladen Mladenov).
NASA: 42/43.
Picture the Past: 10 (Image Courtesy of Derby Museums and Art Gallery and www.picturethepast.org.uk).
Science Photo Library: title page and 19 (Claude Nuridsany & Marie Perennou), 12, 15 (Sheila Terry), 23 top (Charles D. Winters), 24 left, 27, 37 (ISM), 38 bottom (Los Almos National Laboratory), 41.
Shutterstock: 7 (Monkey Business Images), 11 (Mark William Penny), 18 (Alexander Lason), 29 (Stefan Glebowski), 31 (Roman Sigaev), 32 (HomeStudio), 33, 34 (C).

Every attempt has been made to clear copyright. Should there be any inadvertent omission, please apply to the publisher for rectification.

A CIP catalogue record for this book is available from the British Library.

Dewey Decimal Classification Number: 546.8

ISBN 978 1 4451 0054 8

Printed in China

Franklin Watts is a division of Hachette Children's Books, an Hachette UK company.
www.hachette.co.uk

SL001446EN

The IUPAC has recently recommended alternative spellings for the names of some elements and groups of elements, for example sulfur and actinoids. For clarity, we have decided to use traditional spellings in this book.

Contents

Chemical elements

The periodic table

The **periodic table** is a very useful invention for chemists, the scientists who study the substances around us. It is a chart containing all the known chemical **elements**. It even has spaces for elements not yet discovered. To understand the periodic table, how it was invented and why it is needed by chemists, it is important to know a little about **atoms** and elements.

Atoms

Books, birds, buildings and all the other things around you are made from tiny things called atoms. You are made from atoms, too. Atoms are so small that a million of the biggest ones would make a pile less than half a millimetre high. We cannot see atoms, even with a microscope. It can be difficult to believe that something invisible exists. Just over a hundred years ago a few scientists still did not believe in atoms, but the results of many experiments show that atoms are real. Not only that, they are made from even smaller things called **sub-atomic particles**.

Inside an atom

There are three main types of sub-atomic particle. **Protons** and **neutrons** are the heaviest. They join together to make a

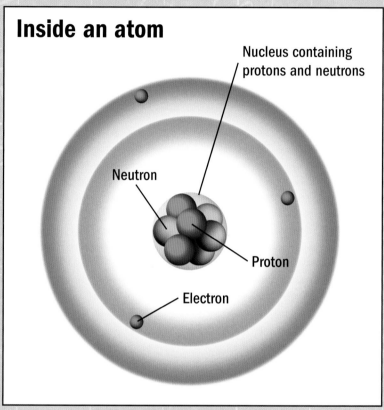

Inside an atom

Nucleus containing protons and neutrons

Neutron

Proton

Electron

This is a diagram of a lithium atom. Its nucleus is surrounded by three electrons, and it contains three protons and four neutrons.

cluster in the middle of the atom, called the **nucleus. Electrons** are much lighter sub-atomic particles, and clouds of them surround the nucleus.

THAT'S A FACT!

The nucleus of an atom is around 100,000 times smaller than the atom as a whole, and most of an atom is empty space. The name 'atom' comes from the Greek word 'atomos', meaning something that cannot be split.

Elements

A chemical element is a substance made from one type of atom. Some elements have been known for thousands of years, such as gold and iron. Others have been discovered much more recently. Helium, used in party balloons, was discovered in 1895. Americium, used in smoke alarms, was only discovered in 1944. Scientists continue to discover new elements today.

The **atomic number** (proton number) of an atom is the number of protons it contains. All the atoms of an element have the same atomic number. Hydrogen and

Everything is made from atoms, even you. Oxygen atoms make up 65 per cent of your body and carbon atoms make up 18 per cent of it. Hydrogen atoms make up most of the rest, along with small percentages of many other elements.

carbon are two different elements. Every hydrogen atom contains just one proton, but every carbon atom contains six protons. There are over a hundred different elements, and no two elements have the same atomic number. The periodic table helps chemists to understand all the different elements and what they do.

The periodic table of elements

A closer look

The periodic table might seem confusing at first, so let's look at its main features. Each box contains information about a single element, such as hydrogen or oxygen. You will not find water or any other **compound** in the periodic table. This is because compounds are made from two or more elements chemically joined together. For example, water is a compound made up of two hydrogen atoms and one oxygen atom.

Chemical symbols

Each element has its own chemical symbol, made from one, two or sometimes three letters. The first letter is always a capital letter, and any others are lower case. Some symbols are easy to understand, such as H for hydrogen and C for carbon. Others, such as Cu for copper, are not so obvious.

THAT'S A FACT!

The ancient Romans had copper mines on Cyprus, an island in the Mediterranean Sea. They called the metal 'aes Cyprium', which became shortened to 'cuprum'. That is why the symbol for copper is Cu and not Co (which is the symbol for cobalt).

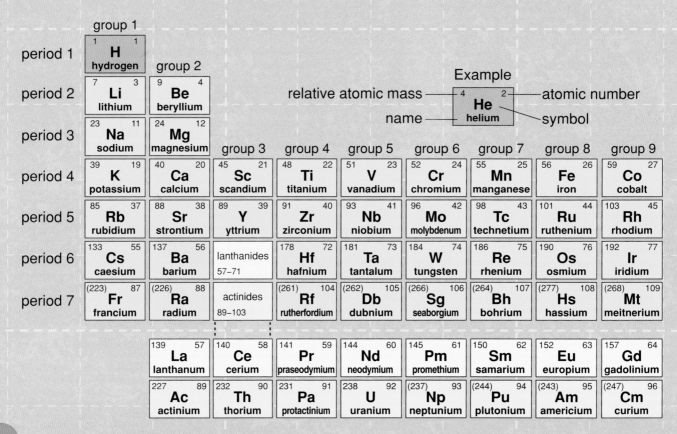

The numbers

Atoms are not only very small, they are also very light. They are so light that it makes little sense to use their actual masses in grams. Instead, their **relative atomic mass** is used. This is the mass of the atom compared to the mass of a carbon atom. Hydrogen atoms are the lightest. Their relative atomic mass is just 1. The relative atomic mass of carbon is 12, so a carbon atom weighs 12 times more than a hydrogen atom. The top left number in each box of the periodic table is the relative atomic mass of the element. The top right one is the atomic number, the number of protons in that element's atoms.

Periods

A horizontal row in the periodic table is called a **period**. The elements are arranged in order of increasing atomic number. As you go from left to right across a period, the atomic number on the right increases by one each time.

Groups

A vertical column in the periodic table is called a **group**. The elements in a group have similar chemical properties. For example, the elements in group 1 are very **reactive** metals. The elements in group 18 are very **unreactive** non-metals. You are going to find out more about elements like these and how understanding them helped in the invention of the periodic table.

The periodic table of elements. The number on the left in each box is the element's relative atomic mass, and the number on the right is its atomic number (proton number).

			group 13	group 14	group 15	group 16	group 17	group 18	
								4 **He** 2 helium	period 1
			11 **B** 5 boron	12 **C** 6 carbon	14 **N** 7 nitrogen	16 **O** 8 oxygen	19 **F** 9 fluorine	20 **Ne** 10 neon	period 2
			27 **Al** 13 aluminium	28 **Si** 14 silicon	31 **P** 15 phosphorus	32 **S** 16 sulphur	35 **Cl** 17 chlorine	40 **Ar** 18 argon	period 3
group 10	group 11	group 12							
59 **Ni** 28 nickel	63.5 **Cu** 29 copper	65 **Zn** 30 zinc	70 **Ga** 31 gallium	73 **Ge** 32 germanium	75 **As** 33 arsenic	79 **Se** 34 selenium	80 **Br** 35 bromine	84 **Kr** 36 krypton	period 4
106 **Pd** 46 palladium	108 **Ag** 47 silver	112 **Cd** 48 cadmium	115 **In** 49 indium	119 **Sn** 50 tin	122 **Sb** 51 antimony	128 **Te** 52 tellurium	127 **I** 53 iodine	131 **Xe** 54 xenon	period 5
195 **Pt** 78 platinum	197 **Au** 79 gold	201 **Hg** 80 mercury	204 **Tl** 81 thallium	207 **Pb** 82 lead	209 **Bi** 83 bismuth	(209) **Po** 84 polonium	(210) **At** 85 astatine	(222) **Rn** 86 radon	period 6
(271) **Ds** 110 darmstadtium	(272) **Rg** 111 roentgenium	(285) **Cn** 112 copernicium	(284) **Uut** 113 ununtrium	(289) **Uuq** 114 ununquadium	(288) **Uup** 115 ununpentium	(293) **Uuh** 116 ununhexium	? **Uus** 117 ununseptium	(294) **Uuo** 118 ununoctium	period 7

Legend:
- metals
- non–metals
- metalloids

159 **Tb** 65 terbium	162 **Dy** 66 dysprosium	165 **Ho** 67 holmium	167 **Er** 68 erbium	169 **Tm** 69 thulium	173 **Yb** 70 ytterbium	175 **Lu** 71 lutetium
(247) **Bk** 97 berkelium	(251) **Cf** 98 californium	(252) **Es** 99 einsteinium	(257) **Fm** 100 fermium	(258) **Md** 101 mendelevium	(259) **No** 102 nobelium	(262) **Lr** 103 lawrencium

Ancient elements

It was difficult to do complex experiments thousands of years ago. In those days, **philosophers** thought carefully about the world and came up with ideas to explain what they saw. Aristotle was a Greek philosopher who was born in 384 BCE. He thought that everything on earth was made from four 'elements'. These were air, earth, fire and water. Aristotle could not prove this but people thought highly of him, so his ideas influenced science for almost 2,000 years. This began to change in the 17th century.

Unlucky for some

Just 13 elements were known in the 1660s. These included non-metals such as carbon and sulphur, and metals such as gold, copper and iron. But because everybody still believed in Aristotle's idea of four 'elements', no one recognized these substances for what they were – true elements.

Alchemy

In 1669, a German **alchemist** called Hennig Brand tried to make gold from urine. Instead he discovered a new element, phosphorus. Alchemy was a strange mixture of chemistry, religion and mystery. One of its aims was to make gold from cheaper substances. Brand's thoughts went along the lines of 'urine is golden coloured, so it might contain gold'.

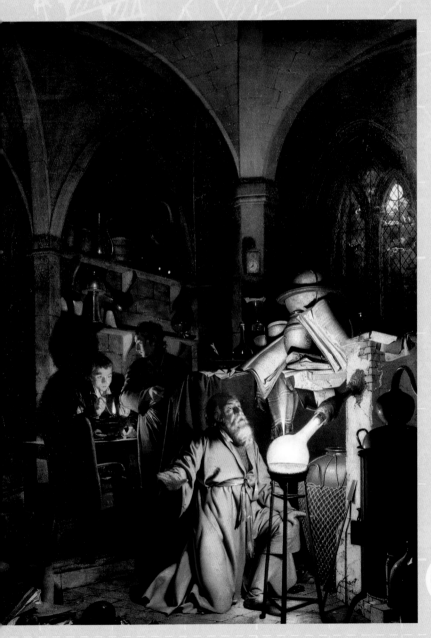

This 1771 painting by Joseph Wright shows an alchemist making phosphorus.

Red phosphorus is a form of phosphorus that catches fire at a higher temperature than white phosphorus. It is used in matches.

Bringer of light

Brand collected fifty buckets of urine. He left them to stand for several days and then heated the stinky sludge to concentrate it. He heated the remaining ghastly goo to evaporate some of it and then cooled the vapour. In this way, Brand used **distillation** to collect a pure, waxy white solid. Once in the air, this gave off a green glow in the dark and it could suddenly burst into flames. It was called phosphorus after the Greek words meaning 'bringer of light'. Brand had discovered that phosphorus is an element found naturally in the body. Our bones contain most of it and any extra comes out in our urine.

Brand never made his fortune from his discovery. Even though he tried to keep his methods secret, other people worked out how to make phosphorus and became rich.

THAT'S A FACT!

Brand was lucky. Had he collected his phosphorus in the open air instead of water, he could have been seriously hurt. White phosphorus does not react with water, but it is very dangerous in air. It can set itself on fire and then burn violently. Today, it is used in incendiary bombs, which cause damage by starting fires.

Breakthrough

Brand's discovery of phosphorus encouraged the search for other new elements. There was a good chance that if a new element could be found through experiments, others could also be found.

The sceptical chemist

Candles and mice

Around the same time as Brand's discovery of phosphorus, John Mayow was experimenting with air. He published his results in 1668. In one experiment, Mayow put a lighted candle in a dish of water and covered it with an up-turned jar. The flame eventually went out and water rose a little inside the jar. If he put a mouse inside instead of a candle, it eventually suffocated and water rose again. Mayow then discovered that a mouse would suffocate faster if there was a lighted candle in the jar as well.

Mayow's experiments do not sound very pleasant, but he had made two important discoveries. He had discovered that flames and living things need the same part of air. Since only some of the air was

John Mayow published some of his results in 1674. These diagrams showed readers how his experiments on air were set up.

Robert Boyle

Date of birth: 25 January 1627

Place of birth: Lismore, Ireland

Greatest achievement: Boyle's book was a turning point in chemistry. His experiments on gas pressure and volume led to Boyle's Law of Gases.

Interesting fact: In 1680, Boyle turned down the chance to be the president of the Royal Society (the world's oldest scientific organization).

Date of death: 31 December 1691

used up and not all of it, he discovered that air must contain at least two different gases. It could not be an element after all. Doubts about Aristotle's four 'elements' were starting to grow.

Towards modern elements

Robert Boyle published a book called *The Sceptical Chymist* in 1661. He discussed the chemical ideas of his day, including those of Aristotle. Boyle noted that blood broke down when heated, forming more than just four substances. On the other hand, gold would not break down at all. By the time the second edition of the book was published in 1680, Boyle had worked out how to make phosphorus himself, and had carried out many experiments on air. Boyle defined an element as a substance that cannot be broken down. He argued that only experiments could show if a substance was an element.

THAT'S A FACT!

Mayow and Boyle were at Oxford University at the same time and it is possible that Mayow did his experiments in Boyle's laboratory. Robert Hooke, a scientist who had once been Boyle's assistant, helped Mayow become a Fellow of the Royal Society.

Breakthrough

Boyle provided the first modern definition of an element. He argued that the ancient idea of four 'elements' was wrong and that experiments are needed to show if a substance is an element.

Mice and men

A breath of fresh air

John Mayow discovered that air contains a gas that we now know is oxygen. But Mayow did not make any or separate it from air, so he did not discover oxygen in the scientific sense.

In 1774, an English clergyman called Joseph Priestley reported that he had discovered a new gas. He called it 'dephlogisticated air', which he made by heating 'red calx of mercury' (which we now know as mercury oxide). A candle would burn more brightly in this new gas than in ordinary air, and a mouse would survive longer in it. He tried breathing it himself and reported that it was 'much better than common air'. Priestley travelled to Paris later that year and met the French chemist, Antoine Lavoisier.

'I consider nature a vast chemical laboratory in which all kinds of compositions and decompositions are formed.'
Antoine Lavoisier

The acid maker

One of Lavoisier's talents was to pull together different pieces of research from other scientists. He carried out his own research after meeting Priestley. He concluded that the new gas was an element, and that it was needed for burning and **respiration**. He also (wrongly) thought it was present in all acids. So he called it oxygen, from the Greek words meaning 'acid maker'.

The natural world consists of many different substances, from simple ones such as water and oxygen, to complex ones such as the cellulose found in these toadstools.

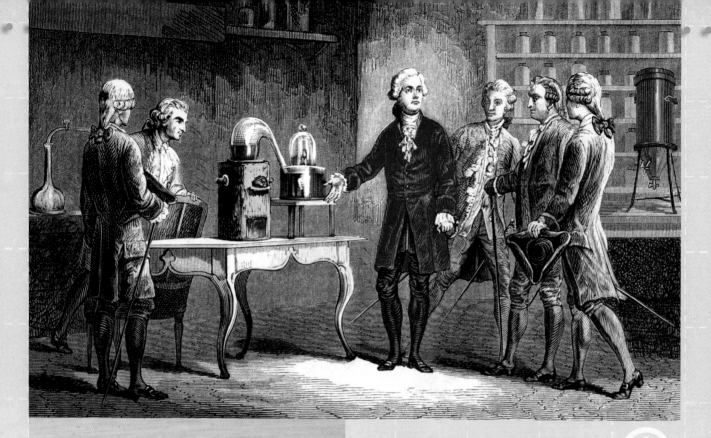

This historical painting shows Lavoisier showing other scientists his experiments on air and oxygen.

Antoine Lavoisier

Date of birth: 26 August 1743

Place of birth: Paris, France

Greatest achievements: Lavoisier co-discovered oxygen, correctly explained how burning works, and made a naming system for chemicals.

Interesting fact: Lavoisier was executed by guillotine as a result of the **French Revolution**.

Date of death: 8 May 1794

example, 'sulphuric acid' replaced 'oil of vitriol', and 'sulphate of copper' replaced 'Roman vitriol'. Lavoisier went further and published his *Elementary Treatise on Chemistry* in 1789. This included Boyle's earlier definition of an element, and also a list of elements. Although he wrongly included light and heat as elements, Lavoisier's work was a great step forward for chemistry.

Towards modern chemistry

Lavoisier worked with three other important scientists to make a sensible system for naming chemicals. This was published in 1787 and replaced older, confusing names for chemicals. For

Breakthrough

Lavoisier successfully linked together ideas from other scientists and set the scene for the development of modern chemistry.

Atoms and symbols

Lost in translation

Here is a **word equation**, written in Polish, for a simple chemical reaction:

$$wegiel + tlen \longrightarrow dwutlenek\ wegla$$

The arrow shows that the substances on the left react to become the substance on the right. Can you work out what the substances are? You are unlikely to be successful unless you understand Polish. Lavoisier's work solved one problem and created another. He made a new naming system, but this was then translated into different languages. So it was still difficult for chemists in different countries to explain their experiments to each other. Chemists needed a way to communicate with each other, whatever language they spoke.

Dalton's chemical symbols and relative atomic masses. He used single letters for some symbols but signs for others.

Dalton's symbols

John Dalton was an English chemist who invented symbols for the elements. He published his *New System of Chemical Philosophy* in 1808. This included a list of twenty elements and their symbols. He even showed how compounds could be represented by joining symbols together. Unfortunately, Dalton's symbols were difficult to learn and to write.

ELEMENTS

Element	w.t	Element	w.t
Hydrogen	1	Strontian	46
Azote	5	Barytes	68
Carbon	54	Iron	50
Oxygen	7	Zinc	56
Phosphorus	9	Copper	56
Sulphur	13	Lead	90
Magnesia	20	Silver	190
Lime	24	Gold	190
Soda	28	Platina	190
Potash	42	Mercury	167

John Dalton was colour-blind. Everything other than blue seemed like shades of yellow to him. Dalton thought that the liquid in his eyes might be blue instead of colourless. He published a scientific paper about it in 1798, and even left instructions that his eyes should be dissected after his death. They were, and the liquid was normal. In 1995, DNA tests on his eyes showed that he only had two types of colour-sensitive cells instead of the normal three.

Letters of distinction

A simpler system was developed in 1819 by Jöns Jackob Berzelius, a Swedish chemist. He gave each element a symbol consisting of one or two letters, based on its Latin name. For example, carbon is C and oxygen is O. Two letters are used if two or more elements have the same first letter. So copper is Cu, cobalt is Co and calcium is Ca. Numbers are used in a **formula** if a substance contains two or more atoms of the same element. For example, oxygen gas is O_2 and carbon dioxide is CO_2.

'Berzelius' symbols are horrifying. A young student in chemistry might as soon learn Hebrew as make himself acquainted with them.'
John Dalton

The system took several decades to be accepted by all chemists. Even Berzelius took some time to use it fully. Perhaps not surprisingly, Dalton hated it. But it does work. Here is that Polish equation, this time written as a **symbol equation**:

$$C + O_2 \rightarrow CO_2$$

Can you tell what the substances are now?

ELEMENTS

H	hydrogen	1	Sr	strontium	88
N	nitrogen	14	Ba	barium	137
C	carbon	12	Fe	iron	56
O	oxygen	16	Zn	zinc	65
P	phosphorus	31	Cu	copper	63.5
S	sulphur	32	Pb	lead	207
Mg	magnesium	24	Ag	silver	108
Ca	calcium	40	Au	gold	197
Na	sodium	23	Pt	platinum	195
K	potassium	39	Hg	mercury	201

Modern chemical symbols and relative atomic masses for Dalton's elements. The reason for some symbols is obvious, such as H for hydrogen, but not obvious for others. For example, the symbol Na for sodium comes from the Latin word 'natrium'. Mercury's symbol, Hg, comes from the Latin word 'hydrargyrum' meaning 'liquid silver'. This is because mercury is liquid at room temperature.

Breakthrough

Berzelius provided chemists with a simple way to describe chemicals and their reactions, using symbols and formulae.

The triads

Organization

When Robert Boyle wrote the second edition of his *Sceptical Chymist* in 1680, just 14 elements were known. By the time Berzelius published his chemical symbols in 1819, the number of known elements had reached 52, almost half the number we know of today. Chemists desperately needed a way to organize the elements.

Dalton and Berzelius help out

Dalton's chemical symbols may not have been successful but his atomic theory was. In those days many scientists did not believe in atoms, and those who did thought that they were probably all the same. Dalton thought differently. He suggested that all the atoms in a particular element were the same, and that different elements were made from different atoms with different masses. He also suggested that atoms join together to make compounds.

Dalton's theory was very similar to the modern one. It was the missing link that Berzelius needed to calculate the relative atomic masses of elements. Dalton also

Sodium burns quickly in the air with a bright orange flame. The light pollution that can be seen around large cities contains sodium vapour.

calculated relative atomic masses, but Berzelius was a more careful worker. He weighed samples of different substances very carefully and his numbers were very precise for the time.

Three by three

During the 1820s, a German chemist called Johann Döbereiner noticed patterns with certain elements. For example, he noticed that lithium, sodium and potassium had similar properties. These are all soft, lightweight but very reactive metals. If they are listed in order of increasing relative atomic mass, they are also in order of increasing reactivity. Chlorine, bromine and iodine are very reactive non-metals. If they are listed in order of increasing relative atomic mass, they are in order of decreasing reactivity.

Döbereiner called such families of three elements **triads**. He noticed that the relative atomic mass of the middle element in each triad was roughly halfway between the other two. Unfortunately, he could not explain his observations.

These are two of Döbereiner's triads. Lithium, sodium and potassium belong in group 1 in the modern periodic table. The other three elements belong in group 17.

Symbol	Name	Atomic mass
Li	lithium	7
Na	sodium	23
K	potassium	39
Cl	chlorine	35.5
Br	bromine	80
I	iodine	127

Iodine is a reactive non-metal. It exists as shiny purple-black crystals at room temperature. When these are warmed, they turn directly into a purple vapour without melting.

Breakthrough

Berzelius provided chemists with precise values for relative atomic masses. Döbereiner's triads were an early attempt to group elements together, and showed that there might be links to their relative atomic masses.

A 3D table

Expanding the triads

Other chemists extended Döbereiner's triads so that they included more than the original three elements. For example, fluorine was added to the top of the triad containing chlorine, bromine and iodine. Other 'triads' were produced, such as one containing oxygen, sulphur, selenium and tellurium. But there was no system linking everything together. One of the problems was that many relative atomic masses were still wrong.

Molecular muddle

Atoms can join together to make **molecules**. The chemical formula for a substance depends upon the numbers of different atoms its molecules contain. Chemists needed correct formulae to work out relative atomic masses. They got many formulae right, but some were wrong. For example, water is H_2O (two hydrogen atoms attached to one oxygen atom) but at the time chemists thought it was HO. Relative atomic masses based on the wrong formula would also be wrong. The problem was solved by two Italian chemists.

In 1811, Amedeo Avogadro discovered that the same volume of any gas contains the same number of molecules under the same conditions. So a litre of hydrogen gas would contain the same number of molecules as a litre of water vapour. This

made it possible to work out correct chemical formulae. Stanislao Cannizzaro understood the importance of this. He published a pamphlet in 1858 explaining how to work out accurate relative atomic masses using Avogadro's ideas.

'It was as though the scales fell from my eyes. Doubt vanished and was replaced by a feeling of peaceful clarity.'
The German chemist Lothar Meyer, after reading Cannizzaro's pamphlet.

The telluric spiral

A French **geologist** called Alexandre-Emile de Chancourtois made a periodic table in 1862. He put the elements in order of

This is a photograph of a telluric spiral. You could only see all the elements on the cylinder by rotating it.

increasing relative atomic mass using the new accurate values. He drew his table on paper wrapped around a cylinder. It formed a spiral with tellurium halfway down, so he called it the 'telluric spiral'.

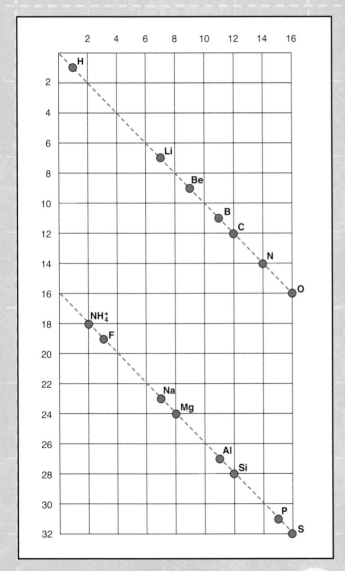

Part of the information on the telluric spiral. The top line does not really stop at O. When the paper is wrapped around a cylinder, it would reappear to the top left of NH$_4$ (which we now know is not an element).

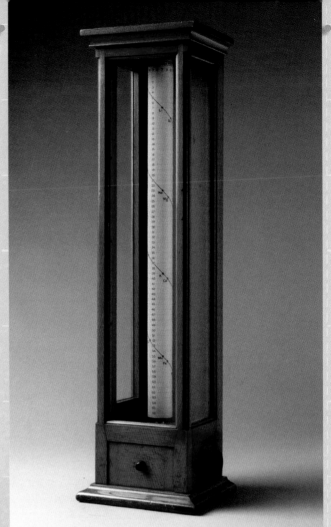

If de Chancourtois made the cylinder 16 mass units around, Döbereiner's triads appeared in vertical columns. The properties of the elements repeated on each turn of the cylinder, too. The telluric spiral should have been received excitedly by other chemists. But it was ignored.

Breakthrough

Cannizzaro's work removed the big variations in relative atomic masses calculated by different chemists. De Chancourtois was the first person to put the known elements in order of increasing relative atomic mass, and he found a repeating pattern.

The Law of Octaves

What next?

Why was the telluric spiral ignored? Some parts showed a **trend** or general change in properties of the elements. But other parts did not. The cylinder was difficult to use. It was even harder to understand because de Chancourtois forgot to put a diagram in his first scientific paper. He remembered later, but few chemists saw it because it was published in a geology journal. Could a chemist do better?

John Newlands

John Newlands, an English chemist, developed a table which he published in 1865. He arranged the known elements in order of increasing relative atomic mass as de Chancourtois had done, but Newlands' table was flat.

'When elements are arranged in increasing order of their atomic mass, the eighth element resembles the first in physical and chemical properties just like the eighth note on a musical scale resembles the first note.'

John Newlands

Newlands called his invention the 'Law of Octaves'. The word 'octaves' comes from the Latin word meaning 'eight'. For Newlands, an octave consisted of an element, the eighth element after it and the six elements in between them. So lithium and sodium are at opposite ends of an octave. Oxygen and sulphur are at opposite ends of a different one. Working

Newlands' Octaves with modern chemical symbols and relative atomic masses. The two triads shown on page 19 are highlighted and extended.

H 1 hydrogen	F 8 fluorine	Cl 15 chlorine	Co cobalt 22 Ni nickel	Br 29 bromine	Pd 36 palladium	I 42 iodine	Pt platinum 50 Ir iridium
Li 2 lithium	Na 9 sodium	K 16 potassium	Cu 23 copper	Rb 30 rubidium	Ag 37 silver	Cs 31 caesium	Os 51 osmium
Be 3 beryllium	Mg 10 magnesium	Ca 17 calcium	Zn 24 zinc	Sr 31 strontium	Cd 38 cadmium	Ba barium 45 V vanadium	Hg 52 mercury
B 4 boron	Al 11 aluminium	Cr 19 chromium	Y 25 yttrium	Ce cerium 33 La lanthanum	U 40 uranium	Ta 46 tantalum	Tl 53 thallium
C 5 carbon	Si 12 silicon	Ti 18 titanium	In 26 indium	Zr 32 zirconium	Sn 39 tin	W 47 tungsten	Pb 54 lead
N 6 nitrogen	P 13 phosphorus	Mn 20 manganese	As 27 arsenic	Di didymium 34 Mo molybdenum	Sb 41 antimony	Nb 48 niobium	Bi 55 bismuth
O 7 oxygen	S 14 sulphur	Fe 21 iron	Se 28 selenium	Rh rhodium 35 Ru ruthenium	Te 43 tellurium	Au 49 gold	Th 56 thorium

in this way, elements with similar properties ended up in the same row. The first column of his table contained the elements hydrogen to oxygen, the same seven elements as the first turn of de Chancourtois' telluric spiral, and Döbereiner's triads appeared in his rows. So had Newlands discovered the right way to order the known elements? Unfortunately not. It only worked as far as calcium. After that things went wrong. For example, iron was in the same row as oxygen and sulphur. Copper, an unreactive metal, was between potassium and rubidium, two very reactive metals. Sometimes he squeezed two elements into one box. So Newlands' invention was not a success.

Newlands put potassium and copper in the same octave. But, unlike copper, potassium reacts violently with water. It burns with a lilac flame and gives off lots of sparks.

Copper is used for roofing because it does not react with water.

That's a Fact!

Criticism of Newlands was unkind. After hearing his ideas at a meeting of the Chemical Society, a scientist mocked Newlands. Hinting that he thought that it was all rubbish, he asked if Newlands had tried putting the elements in alphabetical order instead.

Breakthrough

Newlands' table was a step forward because he not only put the known elements in order of increasing relative atomic mass, but he found a repeating pattern. Although parts of his table were confused, this was the first attempt at a periodic table as we know it.

Joining power

A new way of thinking?

Newlands' table was not a success. He fitted in all the elements known at the time. But new elements continued to be discovered, and he should have left gaps for them. Oddly, he did this in earlier versions of his table and then stopped. And his only reason for choosing seven rows was because that just seemed to work for the first few elements.

Swap shop

A German chemist called Lothar Meyer invented a table in 1864. Just like

de Chancourtois and Newlands, Meyer arranged the elements in order of increasing relative atomic mass. But unlike them, he put the elements into six columns, and he had a good reason.

Each element in one of Meyer's columns had the same joining power, or **valence**. Their atoms could make the same number of chemical joins, or **bonds**. He was so

Lothar Meyer (1830-95) worked on several versions of a periodic table. He was the first person to arrange elements into groups by their valence or joining power.

Valence

Valence is the maximum number of bonds that the atoms of an element can make. For example, hydrogen has a valence of one because its atoms make one bond. Oxygen has a valence of two because its atoms make two bonds. This is why the formula for water is H_2O. A water molecule contains two hydrogen atoms, each joined by one bond to a single oxygen atom.

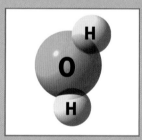

**H_2O (water)
Oxygen has a valence
of two**

**HF (hydrogen fluoride)
Fluorine has a valence
of one**

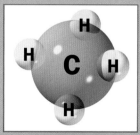

**CH_4 (methane)
Carbon has a valence
of four**

**NH_3 (ammonia)
Nitrogen has a valence
of three**

VALENCE					
4	3	2	1	1	2
				Li 7	Be 9
C 12	N 14	O 16	F 19	Na 23	Mg 24
Si 28	P 31	S 32	Cl 35.5	K 39	Ca 40
? 73?	As 75	Se 79	Br 80	Rb 85	Sr 88
Sn 118	Sb 121	Te 128	I 127	Cs 133	Ba 137
Pb 207	Bi 208			(Tl 204)	

sure that this was the right way to go, he even swapped two elements around. Tellurium has a bigger relative atomic mass than iodine, so it should come first. But Meyer swapped their positions to match their joining power.

Mind the gap

Meyer did something else that was special. He looked at the differences between the relative atomic masses in each column. To keep these the same, Meyer had to shift two elements in the left-hand column down a place. This meant that there might be an element with a relative atomic mass of about 73, waiting to be discovered.

Making **predictions** with good reasons is an important feature of scientific advances, and Meyer's table should have

Meyer's 1864 table. The two triads shown on page 19 are highlighted and extended. Meyer swapped the positions of Te and I to match their joining powers, and he predicted an undiscovered element with a relative atomic mass of 73 (highlighted in red).

been a great success. There was just one problem. It only contained 28 of the 62 elements known at the time, although he did have a go at arranging 22 more in a separate table. The lack of a working table was making life difficult for chemists.

Breakthrough

Meyer's table was a breakthrough because it arranged elements according to relative atomic mass and joining power. He was brave enough to swap two elements to fit this pattern and was able to predict the existence of an element that was not yet discovered.

Mendeleev's first table

Success at last

Dimitri Mendeleev was the Russian chemist who invented the first successful periodic table. This did not happen all at once and he came up with different versions over several years.

Dimitri Mendeleev

Date of birth: 8 February 1834

Place of birth: Tobolsk, Russia

Greatest achievements:
Mendeleev discovered the periodic law and developed the direct ancestor of the modern periodic table.

Interesting facts: Mendeleev was the youngest of 14 brothers and sisters. Mendeleev's family were not wealthy but he was bright and hard-working. He passed his degree at St Petersburg State University in 1855. Mendeleev went to the 1860 international chemistry conference in Karlsruhe, where he met many leading chemists. He later remembered Cannizzaro's pamphlet on relative atomic masses as being particularly important in his research. He became a professor at St Petersburg in 1865. He resigned in 1890 because he disagreed with the way the government was treating university students at the time.

Date of death: 2 February 1907

			K = 39	Rb = 85	Cs = 133	—	—
			Ca = 40	Sr = 87	Ba = 137	—	—
			—	?Yt = 88?	?Di = 138?	Er = 178?	—
			Ti = 48?	Zr = 90	Ce = 140?	?La = 180?	Tb = 231
			V = 51	Nb = 94	—	Ta = 182	—
			Cr = 52	Mo = 96	—	W = 184	U = 240
			Mn = 55	—	—	—	—
Typische Elemente			Fe = 56	Ru = 104	—	Os = 195?	—
			Co = 59	Rh = 104	—	Ir = 197	—
			Ni = 59	Pd = 106	—	Pt = 198?	—
H = 1	Li = 7	Na = 23	Cu = 63	Ag = 108	—	Au = 199?	—
	Be = 9,4	Mg = 24	Zn = 65	Cd = 112	—	Hg = 200	—
	B = 11	Al = 27,3	—	In = 113	—	Tl = 204	—
	C = 12	Si = 28	—	Sn = 118	—	Pb = 207	—
	N = 14	P = 31	As = 75	Sb = 122	—	Bi = 208	—
	O = 16	S = 32	Se = 78	Te = 125?	—	—	—
	F = 19	Cl = 35,5	Br = 80	J = 127	—	—	—

It all started in 1867. In those days you could not get a good chemistry textbook written in Russian. So Mendeleev thought he should write one himself. As he worked on his book, he realized that some elements had similar properties and that it would be really useful to work out a way to organize them.

All in a day's work

Mendeleev made a card for each element. On each one, he wrote the relative atomic mass of the element and information about its properties. He then tried all sorts of ways to organize his cards, swapping them around until he was happy. It only took him a day, but he had been thinking about the problem on and off for years. Mendeleev published his first periodic table in 1869. It contained features from the

Mendeleev published his first periodic table in 1869. He swapped the positions of Te and I, just as Lothar Meyer had done (see the bottom of the fifth column).

tables made by Newlands and Meyer, and included all the known elements. Mendeleev made sure that lots of people knew about his invention. Printed copies of his table were sent to chemists all over Europe.

Breakthrough

Mendeleev's table contained all the known elements in order of increasing relative atomic mass. Each row contained elements with the same joining power, and he swapped elements to suit this pattern. He left spaces for elements not discovered at the time.

Mendeleev's table

Mendeleev's 1869 table was horizontal, with similar elements in rows. He continued working and came up with several versions. He published a detailed explanation of his ideas in 1871. His most famous table was arranged vertically, the same way round as the modern periodic table.

Mendeleev arranged the elements in order of increasing relative atomic mass, just like Newlands and Meyer had done.

A simplified version of Mendeleev's 1871 table. The positions of the predicted elements are highlighted in red. Mendeleev was so sure that Te should come before I (bottom right), he thought its relative atomic mass was only 125.

The horizontal rows were called 'series' and were a bit like the modern periods. Elements with similar properties were in vertical columns. These were called 'groups', just as they are today.

The elements in each group had the same joining power, and this increased from left to right across each series. The chemical formulae at the top of each group are evidence of this. We can look at general formulae where X stands for any element in the group. The numbers in the XO formulae go up in steps of 0.5, and the numbers in the XH formulae go down in steps of 1.

Mendeleev swapped the positions of tellurium and iodine, just as Meyer had

	Group 1	Group 2	Group 3	Group 4	Group 5	Group 6	Group 7	Group 8
Series				XH_4	XH_3	XH_2	XH_1	
	$XO_{0.5}$	XO_1	$XO_{1.5}$	XO_2	$XO_{2.5}$	XO_3	$XO_{3.5}$	XO_4
1	H 1							
2	Li 7	Be 9	B 11	C 12	N 14	O 16	F 19	
3	Na 23	Mg 24	Al 27	Si 28	P 31	S 32	Cl 35.5	
4	K 39	Ca 40	? 44	Ti 48	V 51	Cr 52	Mn 55	Fe 56 Ce 59 Ni 59 Cu 63
5	(Cu 63)	Zn 65	? 68	? 72	As 75	Se 78	Br 80	
6	Rb 85	Sr 87	Y 88	Zr 90	Nb 94	Mo 96	? 100	Ru 104 Ru 104 Pd 106 Ag 108
7	(Ag 108)	Cd 112	In 113	Sn 118	Sb 122	Te 125	I 127	

done. Both men did this to fit the joining power pattern. But Mendeleev went one step further. He thought that the relative atomic mass of tellurium was wrong. So he just changed it from 128 to 125 to fit the pattern in relative atomic masses.

Tellurium is used in the coating of rewritable CDs and DVDs.

A look into the future

Mendeleev spotted gaps in the periodic table. He thought that there must be elements to fit these gaps waiting to be discovered. He made very detailed predictions about what they would be like, based on the elements around each gap. Mendeleev even named them. He used the Sanskrit word 'eka', meaning 'one', to show that each was one place away from a

similar element. The missing elements were 'eka-boron', 'eka-aluminium', 'eka-silicon' and 'eka-manganese'. Did they really exist?

Breakthrough

Mendeleev made detailed predictions about the properties of some undiscovered elements, based on the gaps in his periodic table. There would be strong support for Mendeleev's table if elements with these properties were found.

Three eka elements

Predictions

Mendeleev used his periodic table to predict that there were elements still to be discovered. Would they be discovered? And would they have the right properties to prove that his table worked?

Eka-aluminium

'Eka-aluminium' was discovered in 1875 by Paul-Émile Lecoq de Boisbaudran, a French chemist. He named his discovery gallium. Lecoq did not realize he had found one of Mendeleev's missing 'eka' elements.

When Mendeleev read about gallium, he wrote to the Frenchman. He explained about his predictions for 'eka-aluminium'. These were very close to the actual properties of gallium, except for the melting point. Gallium melts at just 30°C

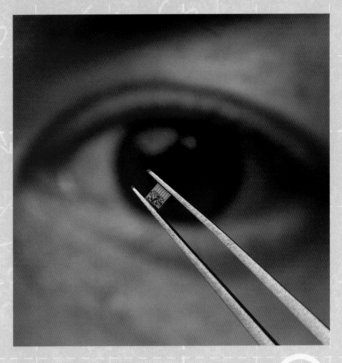

Germanium is used in microprocessors, like this one.

while 'eka-aluminium' was expected to melt between 157°C and 660°C.

THAT'S A FACT!

Was Lecoq de Boisbaudran being cheeky when he named gallium? He said he named it after the Latin word for France. But this is similar to the Latin word for cockerel, and 'le coq' is French for cockerel. So did he actually name gallium after himself? He said no.

Eka-boron

'Eka-boron' was discovered in 1879 by Lars Nilson, a Swedish chemist. He named it scandium because he discovered it in rocks from Scandinavia. Nilson was not looking for any of Mendeleev's missing elements. It was another Swedish chemist, Per Teodor Cleve, who realized that scandium was 'eka-boron' and told Mendeleev. The relative atomic mass of scandium was the same as 'eka-boron', and its other properties were close, too. It was all looking very good for Mendeleev's ideas.

THAT'S A FACT!

Scandium has few uses today. Gallium is used in solar cells, and the flat screens found in most mobile phones and computer monitors. Germanium is used in microprocessors, the tiny 'brains' found in all sorts of electronic equipment.

Eka-silicon

'Eka-silicon' was discovered in 1886 by Clemens Winkler, a German chemist. He named it germanium after Germany. There was some confusion between Mendeleev

Gallium is used in light-emitting diodes or LEDs.

and Winkler. It took them a while to decide that germanium was the missing 'eka-silicon' and not a different eka element. But in the end they agreed that germanium really was the element predicted by Mendeleev many years before.

Breakthrough

The discovery of three of Mendeleev's predicted elements was strong support for his periodic table. Their properties were very close to the properties predicted years before, helping to convince other chemists that his ideas were right.

A whole new group

The search goes on

By the early 1880s, chemists were confident they would find the remaining eka elements and that these would fit nicely into the table. What happened next surprised everyone.

The inactive one

Nitrogen is an unreactive gas that can be separated from air by distillation. An English scientist, Lord Rayleigh, suspected that nitrogen separated like this was not really pure. In 1894, Rayleigh and a Scottish chemist called William Ramsay separated another unreactive gas from nitrogen. They called the new element argon, after the Greek word for 'inactive'. No one had predicted argon and chemists argued about it. Mendeleev worried about how to fit argon into his table. He even

THAT'S A FACT!

Helium was first detected in 1868 in the sun. Although the sun is mostly hydrogen, nearly a quarter of its mass is helium. The helium blocks some of the colours of sunlight and this can be detected on earth. Its name comes from the Greek word 'helios', meaning the sun.

thought it was just a type of nitrogen. Things were about to get worse. In 1895 Ramsay discovered a second unreactive element, helium, in a sample of rock.

A good year for the elements

1898 was a good year for Ramsay. It turned out that his sample of argon was impure and contained three other gases. Working with his assistant Morris Travers, he discovered neon in May, krypton in June and xenon in July. They had found three new elements in just six weeks!

Argon is used in old-fashioned filament lamps and in low-energy lightbulbs like this one.

Xenon is used to make very bright headlights for cars.

A German chemist, Friedrich Dorn, discovered a sixth unreactive gas called radon in 1900. But Ramsay was the first person to separate it, ten years later.

Back to the table

Ramsay suggested that the new elements belonged in a new group on the far right of the periodic table, and Mendeleev agreed. In the end, Mendeleev was pleased with the discovery of these unreactive gases. They fitted nicely into his periodic table, rather than wrecking it. They were called the 'noble gases' because they seemed to be too posh to react with other elements.

group 18

4	2
He	
helium	

20	10
Ne	
neon	

40	18
Ar	
argon	

84	36
Kr	
krypton	

131	54
Xe	
xenon	

(222)	86
Rn	
radon	

The noble gases belong to group 18 on the far right of the periodic table.

William Ramsay

Date of birth: 2 October 1852

Place of birth: Glasgow, Scotland

Greatest achievement: Ramsay is the only person to have been involved in the discovery of an entire chemical group.

Interesting fact: Ramsay was awarded the 1904 **Nobel Prize** in Chemistry 'in recognition of his services in the discovery of the **inert** gaseous elements in air, and his determination of their place in the periodic system.'

Date of death: 23 July 1916

Breakthrough

The ability of the periodic table to fit in an entirely new group of elements gave even more support to Mendeleev's ideas.

Discovering mass

Mendeleev's periodic table had survived the discovery of argon and the other noble gases. But no one could really explain why the elements should be ordered as they were. They were mostly in order of increasing relative atomic mass, although some were swapped around to fit their properties. Chemists used an 'atomic number' for each element but this was just a position in the table. They did not think it was anything you could actually measure. That was about to change in 1913.

Atomic number

Henry Moseley was an English scientist who studied **X-rays**. These are used to take photographs of broken bones, but X-rays can also be used to investigate substances.

Moseley built a machine that produced a beam of electrons. X-rays came off when substances were bombarded by the beam. Moseley analyzed the X-rays that came off

X-rays pass easily through skin but not so easily through bone. Doctors can examine X-ray photographs like this to look for broken bones.

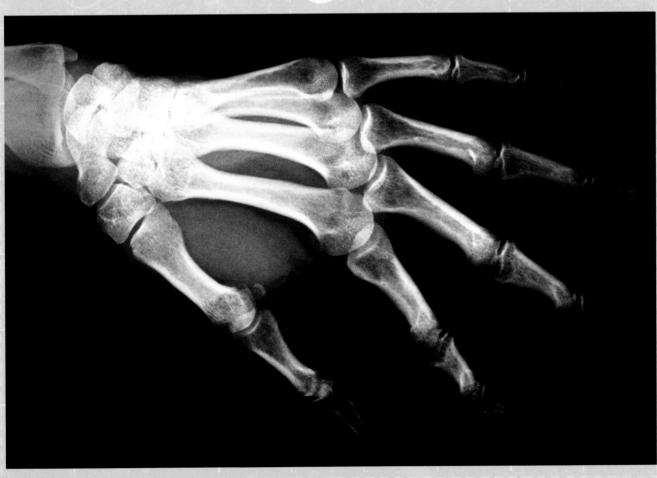

Henry Moseley

Date of birth: 23 November 1887

Place of birth: Weymouth, England

Greatest achievement: Moseley discovered a way to measure the atomic number of an element, called Moseley's Law.

Interesting fact: When World War I started, Moseley chose to join the Royal Engineers instead of staying in Britain as a scientist. He fought at the Battle of Gallipoli in Turkey but was killed by a sniper. Other scientists thought that Moseley might have gone on to win a Nobel Prize if he had lived, but it is only given to people while they are alive.

Date of death: 10 August 1915

14 different elements. If he drew a graph using information based on the X-rays' frequency and the position of the elements in the periodic table, he got a straight line. Moseley had discovered how to measure the atomic number of an element. It turned out to be the number of protons in the element's atoms.

How many?

Moseley's work explained why Mendeleev had to swap the positions of iodine and tellurium. Even though tellurium's relative atomic mass is higher than iodine's, its atomic number is lower. That is why tellurium has to come first. Moseley's work led to the discovery that there could only be 90 elements between hydrogen and uranium, and that there were seven elements still to find.

Moseley's work settled the tellurium-iodine swapping problem. In the modern periodic table, the elements are arranged in order of atomic number, not relative atomic mass, so tellurium comes first.

Breakthrough

Moseley's discoveries using his X-ray machine allowed chemists to link the properties of each element to the particles in its atoms. It also showed that there were still gaps in the periodic table.

Mendeleev's last eka element

Still to be found

Henry Moseley's work showed that seven elements between hydrogen and uranium were left to be discovered. One of these was element 43, the 'eka-manganese' predicted by Mendeleev nearly half a century earlier. Could it be found?

Atom smashing

Ernest Lawrence, an American scientist, invented the **cyclotron** in 1929. The cyclotron is a type of particle accelerator, a machine which can accelerate atoms to very high speeds. The atoms whirl around inside the cyclotron, getting faster and faster, until they smash into a target. An

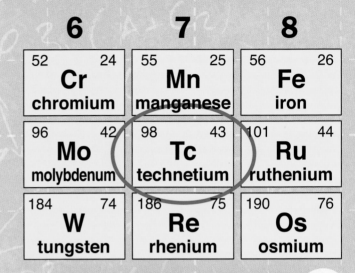

6	7	8
52 24 **Cr** chromium	55 25 **Mn** manganese	56 26 **Fe** iron
96 42 **Mo** molybdenum	98 43 **Tc** technetium	101 44 **Ru** ruthenium
184 74 **W** tungsten	186 75 **Re** rhenium	190 76 **Os** osmium

Technetium, the element placed underneath manganese in the periodic table, was the missing 'eka-manganese'.

atom may be going fast enough to join with an atom in the target, making a new atom with a bigger nucleus. The cyclotron gave scientists a way to actually make new elements.

Eka-manganese

There were several unsuccessful attempts to find 'eka-manganese'. Carlo Perrier and Emilio Segrè eventually found the missing element in 1937. The two Italian scientists analyzed a piece of molybdenum metal from one of Lawrence's cyclotrons.

'Instead of an attic with a few test tubes, bits of wire and odds and ends, the attack on the atomic nucleus has required the development and construction of great instruments on an engineering scale.'
Ernest Lawrence (left)

Technetium is radioactive (see page 38). These medical scans show the front and back views of a person with bone cancer. After an injection of a technetium 'tracer' chemical, the technetium concentrates in the cancerous areas, which show up as red.

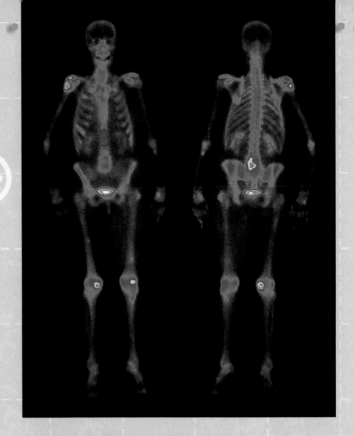

The molybdenum had been bombarded by hydrogen atoms in the cyclotron. Molybdenum atoms have 42 protons and hydrogen atoms have one. Some of the atoms had joined together in the cyclotron to make tiny amounts of an element with 43 protons, the missing 'eka-manganese'. It was named technetium, after the Greek word for 'artificial'. Technetium was the first ever man-made element. There were soon to be many more.

THAT'S A FACT!

Other scientists reported that they had found element 43 before Perrier and Segrè. Walter Noddack, Ida Tacke and Otto Berg thought they had found element 43 in 1925. They called it 'masurium'. They did not get the credit for discovering element 43 because other scientists could not get the same results. But 1925 was not a bad year for the team. They did find rhenium, the missing element 75 predicted by Henry Moseley, and Walter and Ida married each other.

Reactions

Chemical reactions involve electrons in atoms. It is not possible to change an element into a different element using chemical reactions. On the other hand, nuclear reactions involve the nucleus. Nuclear reactions often do cause an element to change into a different one. They happen everywhere naturally all the time. A few will even be happening right now in you. But scientists can make more nuclear reactions happen in their experiments.

Breakthrough

The discovery of technetium filled the last gap in the periodic table predicted by Mendeleev. The invention of machines like the cyclotron allowed scientists to make new elements.

Tweaking the table

Manhattan Project

The Manhattan Project was a secret World War II project. Its aim was to build the world's first atomic bomb. It also led to the world's first **nuclear reactor** and a change to the periodic table.

Uranium

Uranium was discovered in 1789. No one knew then, but uranium atoms can break apart naturally to form smaller atoms. The nucleus gives off nuclear radiation as it breaks apart. This consists of particles and energy fired out from the nucleus. Uranium produces radiation, so it is a **radioactive** substance. Some radioactive substances can be used to make atomic bombs and nuclear

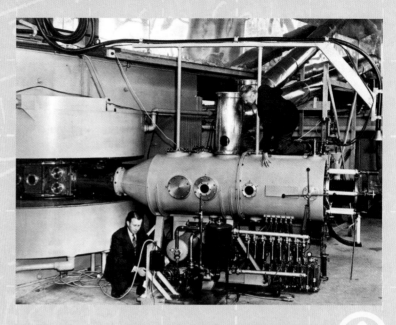

This is the 1.5-m cyclotron built in 1938 by Ernest Lawrence and his team at the Lawrence Berkeley Laboratory in California, USA.

reactors. During the 1930s, scientists began to understand how to make an atomic bomb from uranium.

After the planets

The atomic number of uranium is 92. It is the last natural element in the periodic table found in reasonable amounts on earth. Uranium was named after the planet Uranus. So when element 93 was made in 1940 using a cyclotron, it was named neptunium after Neptune. Element 94 was

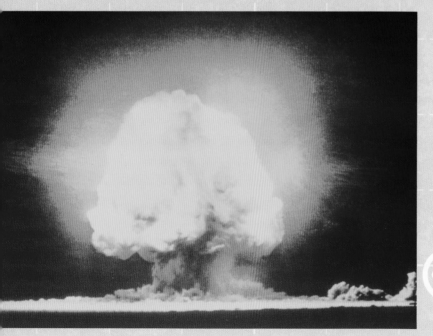

Atomic bombs release huge amounts of energy in a very short time. The first ones used uranium or plutonium.

The world's first nuclear reactor was built under a disused squash court at the University of Chicago in 1942 as part of the Manhattan Project. Uranium was the 'fuel' for the nuclear reaction.

made later that year and was named plutonium, after Pluto. Where would these two elements go in the periodic table?

Even more elements

American scientist Glenn Seaborg was one of the Manhattan Project team who first made plutonium. In 1944, he discovered element 95 (americium) and 96 (curium) in plutonium exposed to radiation in a nuclear reactor. Seaborg found them difficult to separate from other elements.

'I was a 28-year-old kid and I didn't stop to ruminate about it. I didn't think, "My God, we've changed the history of the world!".'
Glenn Seaborg, talking about the discovery of plutonium

The 'transition metals' are the elements placed in the wide block of the periodic table, between groups 2 and 13. One of the transition metals is called tungsten and it has the chemical symbol W. Until the 1940s, uranium was placed in the periodic table immediately below tungsten, where seaborgium is now. Based on this position, Seaborg expected americium and curium to be like transition metals. But they were not. This is why he found

them difficult to separate. So he made an exciting suggestion.

Lanthanides and actinides

The lanthanides are a family of similar metals. They have their own row at the bottom of the table, starting with lanthanum. Seaborg suggested that uranium and the new elements really belonged in another row, underneath the lanthanides. Other elements belonged there, too. This family is called the actinides because the row starts with actinium. This re-arrangement of the table was its last major change.

Seaborg's work led to the last major change in the periodic table. Uranium and other elements were placed in their own row, called the actinides, underneath the lanthanides.

88 38 **Sr** strontium	89 39 **Y** yttrium	91 40 **Zr** zirconium	93 41 **Nb** niobium	96 42 **Mo** molybdenum
137 56 **Ba** barium	lanthanides 57-71	178 72 **Hf** hafnium	181 73 **Ta** tantalum	184 74 **W** tungsten
(226) 88 **Ra** radium	actinides 89-103	(261) 104 **Rf** rutherfordium	(262) 105 **Db** dubnium	(266) 106 **Sg** seaborg

139 57 **La** lanthanum	140 58 **Ce** cerium	141 59 **Pr** praseodymium	144
227 89 **Ac** actinium	232 90 **Th** thorium	231 91 **Pa** protactinium	238 **U** uranium

Breakthrough

Seaborg's discoveries were possible because of nuclear reactions. The periodic table had to be changed because of the new elements discovered by Seaborg.

An agreed design?

Smashing atoms

Research continues in the US, Germany and Russia. Powerful particle accelerators called **linear accelerators** make new atoms by smashing atoms into each other at high speeds. How do scientists cope with the discovery of new elements today?

Naming by number

IUPAC is the International Union of Pure and Applied Chemistry. It is the world's authority for deciding how to name chemicals and their reactions. IUPAC's work involves national chemical societies and chemists from all around the world.

A new element is given a temporary IUPAC name until scientists are sure that it really has been discovered. The name is based on its atomic number and has to end in 'ium', because any new element is likely to be a metal. For example, the temporary name for element 112 is 'ununbium'('un' means 'one' and 'bi' means 'two'). This system can cope with any newly discovered element until it gets a proper name.

'We are being very democratic about naming... We want the name to make sense now and forever – a famous scientist, famous lab, maybe a Greek philosopher.'

Sigurd Hofmann, a leading member of DSI, the German research institute where elements 107 to 112 were first discovered.

Naming for good

The team who discover a new element get the chance to name it. Sometimes two teams discover the same element at the same time or want to use the same name. The agreed name may not suit either team.

Part of a large linear accelerator used by scientists in their research. Sub-atomic particles are accelerated to very high speeds by powerful electric fields, and then smashed into each other to see what happens.

This is an alternative version of the periodic table with the elements arranged like spokes in a wheel, with hydrogen at the centre. Each coloured spoke contains a group arranged in order of increasing atomic number. The transition metals, lanthanides and actinides are arranged in two large clumps at the top.

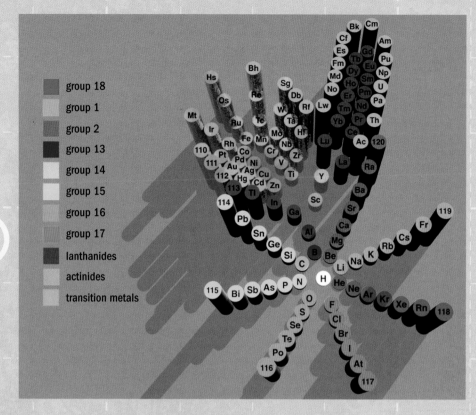

group 18
group 1
group 2
group 13
group 14
group 15
group 16
group 17
lanthanides
actinides
transition metals

For example, the German team who discovered element 107 wanted to name it nielsbohrium, after Danish scientist Niels Bohr. But a Russian team from Dubna wanted that name for element 105. After a lot of argument and discussion, element 105 was named dubnium, and element 107 was named bohrium.

IUPAC allows six months to discuss a new name, in case anyone objects to it. For example, element 112 was named copernicium in 2009, for final agreement in 2010.

IUPAC does not have an agreed design for the periodic table, although in reality the design is settled. People still come up with different designs, including spirals, circles and pyramids. But they are unlikely to catch on.

That's a Fact!

Apart from helium, an element is a metal if its name ends in 'ium'. On the other hand, there are plenty of metals whose names do not end in 'ium', such as gold, iron and platinum. The IUPAC recommended spelling for element 13 is aluminium, as used in the UK, while aluminum (used in the US) is an accepted alternative spelling.

Breakthrough

Powerful linear accelerators have made the discovery of even more new elements possible. The work of IUPAC means that chemists all around the world use the same system for naming elements.

The future

How many elements can there be? Could scientists smash heavier and heavier atoms into each other without limit to get really heavy atoms?

'The aim is to find the end of the periodic table. You can't say where it is until you have tried.'

Sigurd Hofmann (see page 40)

Lots of energy

Atoms need to travel very quickly in particle accelerators to make new superheavy atoms. An atom needs four times more energy just to double its speed. Really heavy atoms would need huge amounts of energy. Today's particle accelerators are powerful, but perhaps in the future even more powerful machines will be built. Then really heavy atoms might be made. Like most superheavy elements, they are likely to be radioactive, with atoms that break apart quickly. But scientists think there might be a small number that will last long enough to perhaps be useful.

During a supernova explosion, material can be flung out at speeds of up to 30,000 kilometres per second. What you see here are the remains of a distant, ancient supernova.

Star dust

About 93 per cent of all the atoms in the universe are hydrogen atoms. Most of the rest are helium atoms. Stars get energy from smashing hydrogen atoms together to make helium atoms. As a star gets older, heavy atoms such as carbon, oxygen and iron atoms gradually build up inside. Old stars can burst in a huge explosion called a supernova.

When a supernova happens, the star's atoms are flung out into space. Over time, new stars and planets can form from these atoms. Most of the heaviest atoms end up in the planets. That is where the heavy atoms on earth came from. You, and everything around you, are made from star dust.

Iron atoms are the heaviest atoms made in a star. Heavier atoms are made in a supernova. Is it possible that superheavy atoms are made in the explosion? It seems that even a supernova is not powerful enough. This is why superheavy elements are not found naturally on earth. Instead, they must be made inside high-energy particle accelerators, just a few atoms at a time.

Falling apart

The number of particles in a nucleus must be just right. The nucleus will fall apart if there are too few neutrons compared to its protons, or too many. Scientists have worked out that the heaviest atom possible should have an atomic number of 155. So is that it?

Fitting in

Making really superheavy atoms will be very difficult, but scientists will try. Perhaps in the future all the gaps in the periodic table will be filled as far as element 155. And maybe past it. Remember that no one predicted the noble gases. However many elements there really are, it is likely that the periodic table will fit them in just nicely.

THAT'S A FACT!

Our sun is just one of about 10 billion stars in our galaxy, the Milky Way. When a supernova happens, the explosion releases more energy than our sun will do in its entire life. A supernova can be brighter than all the stars together in its galaxy.

Glossary

alchemist someone who does alchemy, an early sort of chemistry

atom small particle from which all substances are made

atomic number the number of protons in an atom

bond chemical join between two atoms

compound substance made from two or more elements chemically joined together

cyclotron a type of particle accelerator in which the particles move in a spiral

distillation method used to separate substances by boiling then condensing

electron particle surrounding the nucleus of an atom

element substance made of one type of atom

formula(e) sign for a substance made from two or more atoms

French Revolution A time from 1789 to 1799 when there was a lot of social and political change in France, including the killing of the king and queen

geologist scientist who studies the earth and its rocks

group vertical column in the periodic table

inert does not react easily

linear accelerator a type of particle accelerator in which the particles move in a straight line

molecule particle made from two or more atoms joined together

neutron particle found in the nucleus of an atom

Nobel Prize international prize awarded each year for special success in chemistry, physics, medicine, literature, economics and peace

nuclear reactor machine in which nuclear reactions can run safely. Nuclear power stations use the heat from nuclear reactors to generate electricity.

nucleus central part of an atom

period horizontal row in the periodic table

periodic table chart that arranges elements. In the modern periodic table, elements are organized in atomic number order.

philosopher someone who thinks about how natural things might work

prediction in science, an idea about what will happen next, with a reason

proton particle found in the nucleus of an atom

radioactive able to give off nuclear radiation

reactive able to take part in chemical reactions easily

relative atomic mass the mass of an atom compared to the mass of a carbon atom

respiration chemical reaction in living cells that releases energy

sub-atomic particle object smaller than an atom

symbol equation a way of showing what happens in a chemical reaction using chemical symbols and formulae

trend general increase or decrease

triad family of elements with similar properties, originally containing three elements but later four or more

unreactive does not react easily with other substances, if at all

valence the maximum number of chemical bonds made by the atoms of an element

word equation a way of showing what happens in a chemical reaction using words

X-ray a beam of energy that can pass through solid things

Further information

Books

The Periodic Table series by Nigel Saunders. Heinemann Library, 2004 and 2005.

The Periodic Table: Elements with Style by Adrian Dingle. Kingfisher, 2007.

It's Elementary! by Robert Winston. Dorling Kindersley, 2007.

Nature's Building Blocks: An A-Z Guide to the Elements by John Emsley. Oxford University Press, 2003.

The Elements: A Visual Exploration of Every Known Atom in the Universe by Theodore Grey. Black Dog and Leventhal Publishers, 2009.

Some useful web sites

WebElements™
www.webelements.com
Lots of information about each element in the periodic table, including its history, uses, properties and chemical reactions.

Chemicool Periodic Table
www.chemicool.com
An interactive periodic table with detailed information about each element and its properties.

Periodic Table Games
www.rsc.org/education/teachers/learnnet/ptdata/games
Periodic table activities from the Royal Society of Chemistry.

History of the Periodic Table
www.rsc.org/education/teachers/learnnet/periodictable
More from the Royal Society about the history and development of the periodic table.

Dynamic Periodic Table
www.ptable.com
Interactive periodic table with links to videos and photographs of the elements.

Periodic Table: Formulations
www.meta-synthesis.com/webbook/35_pt/pt.html
Information about all sorts of different designs of periodic tables.

Index